Marxism and Women's Liberation

Katherine Connelly, Elaine Graham-Leigh, Feyzi Ismail
and Lindsey German

COUNTERFIRE

Marxism and Women's Liberation

First published in Great Britain in 2016 by Counterfire, Bow
House, 157 Bow Road, London E3 2SE.
Cover design and layout: Feyzi Ismail

ISBN 978-1-907899-06-5

A catalogue record for this book is available from the British
Library.

Printed and bound in Great Britain.

www.counterfire.org

Contents

1. The fight for women's liberation   5
Katherine Connelly

2. Where does sexism come from?   13
Elaine Graham-Leigh

3. Race, class and women's oppression   31
Feyzi Ismail

4. Marxism and feminism   45
Lindsey German

Further reading   57

About the authors   59

1. The fight for women's liberation

Katherine Connelly

Struggles against women's oppression have typically emerged at times when mass movements have threatened the power of the ruling elites and dreamed of organising society anew.

When the English Revolution 'turned the world upside down', and executed the king for treason against the people, women joined in the ferment of radical ideas, challenging the old restrictions by speaking in public, preaching at meetings, while those who aligned with the most democratic revolutionaries, the Levellers, partook in petitioning and demonstrations.

The French Revolution that began in 1789, in which crowds of ordinary women played a hugely important role, inspired Mary Wollstonecraft's pioneering text *A Vindication of the Rights of Woman*.[1] Wollstonecraft compared the useless, ornamental role which was socially expected of upper-class women to the illegitimate power of the aristocracy and called for women to be educated according to the revolutionary ideals of equality and reason. The revolutionary assault on tyranny provided Wollstonecraft with a language for resistance.

Likewise, the abolitionist movement against slavery informed the campaigners for women's suffrage in America and Britain, whilst the militant suffragette movement coincided with campaigns for provision for the unemployed, for working-class representation and Irish self-determination.

In the 1960s, the women's liberation movement named itself accordingly in reference to the influence of the proliferation of national liberation struggles against imperialism, from which it derived inspiration along with the civil rights movement in the United States and, particularly in Britain, the trade union movement.

Understanding the advances made for women's rights in context enables us to see the systemic nature of women's oppression; when the old order, with its old certainties and prejudices, are under attack and a different kind of society is being fought for, it is easier to imagine that we might be able to create a society without oppression. Conversely, at times when the status quo appears all-powerful, it is harder to imagine a different world, and oppression seems an inevitable, depressing and unchanging feature of society.

One of the important contributions that Marx and Engels made in their work on oppression, culminating in Engels' *The Origin of the Family, Private Property and the State*, was to provide a history of women's oppression.[2] By examining the ways that women's oppression, and the role of the family, had changed over time and place according to the structure of society and the interests of its ruling elite, they demonstrated that oppression was not inevitable but was instead socially produced.

The nature of women's oppression has even changed considerably according to the changing shape of capitalism. In the first half of the twentieth-century women were expected to give up work after getting married, pregnancy outside of marriage was widely stigmatised as morally shameful (for the woman), contraceptive methods unreliable and abortion illegal. By the end of the century, women were expected to work after marriage and, while the range of jobs that women were working has vastly increased from those of the mid-twentieth-century, women now disproportionately find themselves in low-wage jobs, at a time when neoliberal capitalism has made work far more insecure and trampled over hard-won workers' rights. Today, attitudes to marriage and sex have changed enormously, allowing women greater freedom, but while in the past women's sexuality was denied or castigated as shameful women today are subject to sexualised objectification which through entertainment, the media, the leisure activities targeted at women, and the "sell yourself" jobs market seems to pervade and distort all aspects of women's lives.

Oppression therefore plays a particular, systemic role in capitalism. Capitalism is a system that works in the interests of a small minority, by exploiting the many. Under capitalism most people have to sell their ability to work in exchange for a wage in order to live. However, the worker does not receive in payment the value of that work – manifestly not: some of the most valuable jobs (childcare, care for the elderly and sick, cleaning) are among the worst paid. The worker does not receive the value of what they produce because before the wage appears in the bank, the profit from it has been taken by the employer (the person who has not done the work). To maintain such gross inequality requires divisions to be imposed within the majority to prevent that majority from turning collectively on the power of the elite. One means of doing this is by forcing the majority to compete against each other for jobs. Oppression is another means.

Marx examined the way that oppression divided workers and diverted them from uniting against the class that was exploiting them when he wrote on the racist oppression of Irish people in nineteenth-century Britain:

> *Every industrial and commercial centre in England now possesses a working class divided into two* hostile *camps, English proletarians and Irish proletarians. The ordinary English worker hates the Irish worker as a competitor who lowers his standard of life. In relation to the Irish worker he regards himself as a member of the* ruling *nation and consequently he becomes a tool of the English aristocrats and capitalists against Ireland, thus strengthening their domination* over himself. *He cherishes religious, social, and national prejudices against the Irish worker. His attitude towards him is much the same as that of the "poor whites" to the Negroes in the former slave states of the U.S.A. The Irishman pays him back with interest in his own money. He sees in the English worker both the accomplice and the stupid tool of the* English rulers in Ireland.

> *This antagonism is artificially kept alive and intensified by the press, the pulpit, the comic papers, in short, by all the means at the disposal of the ruling classes. This* antagonism *is the secret of the* impotence of the English working class,

despite its organisation. It is the secret by which the capitalist class maintains its power. And the latter is quite aware of this.[3]

Marx explained that the propagation of anti-Irish racism not only enabled the exploiting class to intensify the exploitation of Irish workers by paying them less and treating them poorly, it also increased their power over English workers who blamed Irish workers for their lowered standard of living rather than the capitalist class.

Therefore, although oppression targets groups that cross class boundaries (women, black people, LGBT people, disabled people, etc.) and is often experienced individually, understanding that it is maintained by a system that relies and functions on inequality, on a society divided by exploiters and exploited, provides us with an insight into how to fight against oppression.

It means, for example, that although of course it is a consequence of racism and sexism that the top of society is dominated by rich, white men, getting individual women or black people to 'lean in' at the top, to manage the IMF, the EU or global corporations, is not going to solve the problem for the rest of us or indeed get rid of oppression. It is an ineffective kind of feminism that cares only who sits around the boardroom table but does not notice those who clean the boardroom and that they are likely to be low paid women from ethnic minority backgrounds.

However, it is precisely because oppression is experienced across the boundaries of social class, however, that movements against oppression are often divided between a focus on breaking down barriers at the top of society and challenging the oppressive structures of society itself. The militant suffragette movement at the beginning of the twentieth-century is a useful example of the implications of this division.

The Women's Social and Political Union (WSPU), founded by Emmeline and Christabel Pankhurst in 1903, rapidly distanced itself from its radical origins as its leadership increasingly argued that women, no matter what their social position, had more in common with each other than with men of the same class. It was, however, impossible to remove class interests from a campaign waged in a bitterly class-divided society, and in practice it justified the rejection of all demands for wider social change, since these were primarily of interest to working women, and resulted in the marginalisation of working women from the campaign under the pretext that they could be (better) represented by their richer 'sisters'.

The interests that dominated the campaign were starkly revealed with the outbreak of the First World War, when the leadership of the WSPU suspended their campaign for votes for women and instead pledged women's support for the war effort, prioritising defence of the British Empire over women's rights.

A thoroughly different approach was adopted by Sylvia Pankhurst, Christabel's younger sister and fellow militant suffragette. Far from marginalising working-class women, Sylvia Pankhurst organised primarily amongst working women in order to ensure that the struggle for the vote would translate into a struggle for the transformation of the vast majority of women's lives, that winning the vote should not be an acceptance of women into the status quo but ought instead to represent an assault on poverty, low wages, dangerous working conditions, extortionate rents, poor housing and the discrimination that women faced every day.

She therefore also linked the struggle for votes for women with the huge contemporary movement termed the 'Great Unrest', in which workers across the country organised and struck to demand better pay, conditions and treatment at work. Indeed, Sylvia Pankhurst was expelled from the WSPU after she stood on a platform with, and pledged the solidarity of the suffragette movement to, victimised Irish trade unionists, Irish republicans and representatives of British labour organisations in 1913. Sylvia Pankhurst saw not only that these movements faced opposition and violence from the same government, but that working people, precisely because they did all the work in society, had the power to collectively bring the country to a standstill and that they had a shared interest in overcoming the divisions of racism, nationalism and sexism in order that this power could be realised and a fundamental transformation of society achieved.

As with the suffragette movement, the lesson of every struggle against oppression has been that relying upon an elite few to obtain powerful positions has never won fundamental change for the vast majority of people. The significant social changes, the triumphs over oppression, have been achieved when ordinary people have united to challenge that elite and the divisive system that they rely upon.

Notes

1. Mary Wollstonecraft in Janet Todd and Marilyn Butler (eds.), *The Complete Works of Mary Wollstonecraft* (London 1989).
2. Frederick Engels, *The Origins of the Family, Private Property and the State* (London 1972).
3. https://www.marxists.org/archive/marx/works/1870/letters/70_04_09.htm

2. Where does sexism come from?

Elaine Graham-Leigh

The question of the origins of sexism is key to understanding how to fight for women's liberation, yet it is not undisputed. One issue with feminist campaigns that concentrate on the sexist harassment experienced by women in daily life, such as Everyday Sexism,[1] the Hollaback campaigns[2] and so on, is that they carry with them an implication that sexism is primarily located in the minds and the behaviour of individual men, whose attitudes are what women must struggle to change. Even when women's oppression is recognised as systemic, embedded within and arising from the structures of society, explanations for the existence of those structures are various. A clear understanding of the origins of women's oppression, however, is essential to appreciate the role it plays in capitalist exploitation. Women's main enemies are not individual men but the system of oppression from which the bourgeoisie benefits. Women's oppression is rooted in the class society that has existed for thousands of years, and has been shaped by the priorities of that class society.

No such thing as brain sex
Defences of women's oppression on the grounds of women's innate defectiveness have a long and ignoble history. For Victorian scientists, it was the supposed

smaller sizes of women's brains which made them unfit for responsibilities outside the home (supposed because women do not, in fact, have smaller brains than men when their generally smaller body sizes are taken into account). In the twentieth and twenty-first centuries, the biological determinist argument has shifted from the size of women's brains to their internal structures. A range of works, popularised in titles like *Men Are From Mars, Women Are From Venus*, or *Why Men Don't Listen and Why Women Can't Read Maps*, make the case that men's and women's brains have evolved to work in different ways. In this argument, differences in brain structure mean that men and women inherently have different skills, such as logical thinking and problem solving for men, and nurturing and communicating for women, which mean that they are suited to different roles in society.

Peppered as these arguments are with references to neural imaging and new discoveries about brain structure, they can be taken as presentations of scientific fact rather than as tools of women's oppression. However, their conclusions are neither as unassailable nor as objective as supporters of these views would like to make out. In the first place, there is a frequent but erroneous tendency in popularisations of all sorts of scientific arguments, not just those on differences between the sexes, to look at particular symptoms or behaviour and conflate 'located in the brain' with 'is real, involuntary and innate'. There are real problems with this, not least of which is that it relies ultimately on seeing us all as ghosts in the machine: the brain is where the biologically-determined stuff happens, but our personalities, the results of our individual experiences, float disembodied around it.

This is of course nonsense: everything we think takes place in the brain because we don't exist separately from our material reality. The structure of our brains is developed by our experiences, not the other way around.[3] Thus a study which might find that male maths professors had more activity in regions of the brain associated with logical thought than women who described themselves as bad at maths would undoubtedly be reported in some quarters as evidence that men are innately better at maths than women. However, the effect of a sexist culture telling the women that they were doomed to be bad at maths would be effects on the physical reality of their brains: there is nowhere else for these effects to be felt. The comparison of the male and female brains here might tell you that a difference in mathematical ability might exist, but it would tell you nothing about the reasons for it.

In any case, when carefully evaluated, the evidence of various scientific studies on male and female performance and abilities is that there is surprisingly little difference between the sexes in tasks, from communication to map-reading, which are socially gendered. Social permission for men to assume obliviousness to women's verbal cues has not actually deprived them of their ability to understand oral communication (like cats, they understand what we say just fine, they just choose to ignore it).[4] Nor has the persistent denigration of women's abilities in maths and science rendered us unable to think logically, although it does make it much more difficult for our talents in these areas to be recognised and rewarded.

As Cordelia Fine points out in *Delusions of Gender*,[5] many of the apparent differences between the sexes, identified by the studies on which the inherent-differences argument relies, are creations of a far too sensitive protocol for what 'significant activity' in the brain means. When, as she cites, researchers using this protocol were able to detect 'significant activity' in the brain of a dead fish being shown 'emotionally-charged images', this suggests that there is a problem with the design of these studies. She also shows how priming study participants can have a significant effect on how they perform: remind men going into a study, for example, that men are supposed to be bad at interpreting emotions in others and they will perform badly in the test. If you tell them that this is a test on which men usually do well, they will too.

In fact, despite the considerable industry devoted to brain-sex differences, there is very little evidence for significant variances in abilities between men and women as categories. That this is the case in the fundamentally sexist system in which we live is quite remarkable and surely destroys any notion that there are differences between men and women's abilities which are biological and innate. There is clearly no such thing as brain sex, and so no defence of sexism in the structure of our brains.

Prehistoric sex divisions – all about the hunting?

If sexism does not arise from differences in our brains, perhaps it developed because of differences in brawn? It is of course true that men in general can be taller and stronger than women (although in any population, some women will be larger than some men, as there is a considerable degree of overlap).

Add the undeniable fact of women's childbearing role, and for some you have the origins of women's oppression, in the physical realities that underlay the division of labour far back in human history, in the Paleolithic era (otherwise known as the Stone Age).

Arguments about the division of labour in human pre-history are always complicated by the scantiness of our evidence for pre-historic social construction. This means that authoritative pronouncements on the sex-based division of labour are often relying on two problematic sets of assumptions. One comprises the sexist views held by those making the arguments about male and female innate predispositions. Descriptions of women in the Paleolithic that make them sound like 1950s housewives are unfortunately likely to have been inspired by male ideas of 1950s housewives. The other set is rooted in the racist notion that modern hunter-gather societies can function as a time machine back to the Stone Age; that if a society works in a different way from modern Western societies, it is stuck at a past point in human history and can tell us accurately how human societies worked at that time.[6] Neither of these assumptions provide safe or reasonable bases for the reconstruction of Paleolithic gender relations, but underlie many of the arguments for the origins of women's oppression.

The argument for women's oppression arising out of the division of labour is broadly that women's reproductive role meant that they were excluded from the highest-valued types of food production and so acquired a lower status than men as a group. This is not an argument about the amount of productive work carried out by women. Despite childbearing, it's quite usual in agricultural societies for women to be found doing most of the work, and indeed this view also tends to have women providing most of the food for their hunter-gatherer societies, by being the ones responsible for the gathering. While the plant food collected by women might have formed the bulk of Paleolithic diets, however, the argument goes, the most important food was meat, obtained by men on hunting trips from which women were excluded because of their need to take care of the children. In some versions of the argument, bringing home the bacon enabled men to trade it for women's sexual submission. In other versions, it simply gave men as a group a higher status than the women whom biology forced to stay at home.[7] Either way, men, as controllers of the meat supply, were clearly in a potentially privileged position compared to women.

Because labour and the work enabling the reproduction of labour are both heavily gendered in our society, it's easy to assume that such tasks must also have been divided according to sex in human prehistory. In fact, while it is likely that there were sex roles, it is difficult to find a type of work which has consistently belonged to the same sex throughout human society. Growing, gathering and processing plants for food, for example, has been both a female job and a quintessentially male activity. It is therefore not safe to assume that the recent identification of a particular sort of work with either men or women means that it was always so identified.

Hunting does manage to appear particularly male, and there is a common sense argument that women would have been too precious a resource to risk on such dangerous activity. This is potentially convincing, if we're talking about big-game hunting, but this isn't as clear cut as it might appear. There was a movement among palaeontologists in the 1950s and 1960s to see hunting as the 'master behaviour pattern of the human species'.[8] One result of the numerous 'Man the Hunter' conferences to which this movement gave rise has perhaps been an automatic conflation between the human need for protein and bands of courageous Stone-Age men bringing down mammoths. In fact, it is likely that most Paleolithic humans got the vast bulk of their protein either from small animals like rabbits, or from fish and shellfish. Since neither trapping rabbits nor picking mussels off rocks are usually hazardous activities, there is no reason to suppose that women would have been excluded from them. This rather punctures the notion that women's oppression arose from prehistoric man's control of the meat supply. Insofar as we can tell, that control is more wishful thinking by twentieth-century palaeontologists than reality.

The class origins of women's oppression

The idea that Stone-Age men were buying women's sexual submission with aurochs steaks also ignores the fact that these early human societies would have been egalitarian. Individuals would most likely not have been hunting and gathering for themselves, but contributing whatever they got to the communal food supply. The idea that some people could have power over others through the control of specific resources is one that could only come from within a class society, which these early human societies were not. When class societies did start to develop, following the Neolithic agricultural revolution which began in the Middle East around 11,000 years ago, it was this that enabled the development of women's oppression.

Frederick Engels analysed how this came about in his 1884 work *The Origins of the Family, Private Property and the State*.[9] The shift from hunting and gathering to farming, with concomitant developments in things like metallurgy and animal husbandry, meant that human societies could amass many more resources than had previously been possible. Greater material prosperity, however, created the conditions for private property. Once private property was built up by a household, this provided the basis for the idea that property should be heritable. If men wanted to ensure that their property could be inherited by their biological children only, they had to be able to control the women with whom they wanted to produce their children, otherwise they could never be sure of their paternity. Thus developed the patriarchal family, with a man at the head and the women as chattels. It was, as Engels said, 'the historic defeat of the female sex', but it is important to note that it was always for the benefit of the comparatively small number of men who controlled the bulk of the private property in these early class societies. The patriarchal model of the family might have spread to poorer households – if nothing else, it gave the responsibility for supporting poor women and children to the poor men who owned them – but the system benefited only the wealthy, not all men equally.

This description of how material conditions allowed the development of class society might make it sound as if it was inevitable: that women's oppression would always be the consequence of any level of material prosperity and that the alternative would be living in caves. Fortunately, however, this is not the case. Class and women's oppression were not the inescapable result of agriculture but historical events which, if we could go back in time and run the tape again, might well play out differently.

Societies without class and sexism

It is also important to note that while we talk about the development of class society as if this was one phenomenon, the imposition of class on previously egalitarian societies took an extremely long time. In much of western Europe, for example, communal structures at village level long retained facets of Neolithic communism. There was a residual egalitarianism within village societies which feudal lords, with the help of the Church, were only breaking down in the medieval period. Right from the beginning, class was frequently contested. The Neolithic was not only a period of class formation, it was a period of class struggle, in which those who wanted to amass private property, and subjugate those who did not have it, did not get it all their own way.

This is shown clearly in the archaeological record of the Neolithic. In southern Anatolia, for example, the towns which grew up as a result of the development of agriculture start off with all the hallmarks of a particularly nasty class society. They have areas of large houses and other areas best described as slums, huge temples looming over the residential parts, and piles of skulls and traces of blood on temple stones that may suggest a rigid hierarchy kept in place by human sacrifice. Then, in around 7300BC, in the town of Cayönü, something changed. The large houses were burnt down, so quickly that the owners were unable to rescue their goods, and the temple was set on fire and razed to the ground. The slum areas were also cleared and a new town built where the rich area had been, containing only large houses with no size differences between them. The people of Cayönü had made the world's first successful revolution.

The egalitarian society created by the Cayönü revolution seems to have spread to other Anatolian towns, most notably Catal Hüyük, a town of around 1,500 houses built along egalitarian lines, with no sign of class differences. It is particularly notable that while there was no class structure in Catal Hüyük, people also don't seem to have been restricted according to their sex. Unlike men and women in class societies, women in Catal Hüyük could be buried with trade markers like mason's tools, and men were as likely as women to be buried with jewellery. Paintings preserved in the ruins of Catal Hüyük also show men as well as women playing with children, implying that care for small children was not reduced to 'women's work.' Far from being a temporary escape from innate human tendencies to class and women's oppression, these egalitarian societies lasted for more than 3,000 years.[10]

The example of Catal Hüyük shows that neither class society nor women's oppression is a necessary feature of complex human societies. There are also other examples from much more recent periods. Engels cited the Haudenosaunee (which he referred to as the Iroquois), a polity in the north east of the US which existed from around 1000AD until its destruction by white settlers. Haudenosaunee was not a class society and had democratic structures, including the second-oldest continuously-existing parliament in the world.[11] Engels did not entirely recognise the extent to which the democratic nature of Haudenosaunee society also meant equality for women, but it was an inspiration to nineteenth-century US feminists as a demonstration that women did not have to be subjugated. While the war leaders of the Haudenosaunee clans were always male, the clan heads, who were in charge of implementing the democratic decisions for internal government, were always female. Women who were not clan heads had an equal and respected place in the society: as the Great Law put it, members of the democratic council had to make sure to heed 'the warnings of your female relatives.'[12]

Catal Hüyük and Haudenosaunee show that it is possible to have advanced human societies without class and therefore also without women's oppression. Women's oppression is not an innate, unchanging result of human brain structures or human bodies, but a result of the historical development of class. In the same way, the form that women's oppression takes in class societies is also neither constant nor immutable, but changes according to the needs of the ruling class in any particular mode of production. The way in which women are oppressed under capitalism is different from how they were oppressed in ancient states, or under feudalism, because women's oppression is not an inescapable fact of gender relations but a historical phenomenon.

Women's oppression under capitalism

It is the historical nature of women's oppression that explains the varying degrees to which women have been able to escape total domination by men in different societies. The comparatively high status of women in Anglo-Saxon England, for example, compared to their position under the Normans, or the ability of women in the south of France in the medieval period to inherit property and in some cases even exercise political power, are demonstrations of this. When we talk about women's oppression under capitalism, therefore, we have to be aware that we are talking about an oppression that takes the forms it does in order to best suit the needs of the capitalists, not an unchanging oppression inherent in the same form to all class societies.

Under capitalism, the site of production changed from the household, where it had been under feudalism, to the factory. Goods from clothes to cheese were no longer being produced at home, but were made on an industrial scale for those who could afford them. This shift meant that working-class women themselves could no longer be confined to the household, but along with their children were needed to provide cheap labour for the factories. Because for modern feminism being able to go out to work is a key liberty for women, it might be easy to see women's shift from home to factory as an advance, but the conditions under which it occurred made it anything but. Women who fought alongside working men against this and for a family wage for the men were not fighting for their oppression but for a system that would give their children a chance to survive.

The terrible experience of industrialisation in the first half of the nineteenth-century showed that employers could not simply work their existing employees to death without thinking about how their labour would be reproduced, or eventually they would find themselves lacking a next generation of workers. Since state intervention to pay for childcare and housework while working-class women were at work would have been unthinkable, the creation of the patriarchal nuclear family was the only option. This social institution, in which the man went out to work and the woman stayed at home, was a way to provide for the reproduction of labour by building on the existing understanding of household matters and childcare as women's work. This, as Lindsey German points out, 'set the pattern for the working-class family for around 100 years'. It was set not by men invested in patriarchal control of their families but by the needs of the capitalists.[13]

Similarly, more recent shifts in women's ability to work outside the home can also be traced not to the desires of men but to the requirements of the capitalist system. An example here would be the retreat from employment into early marriage and house-wifehood after the Second World War, described by Betty Friedan in *The Feminine Mystique*.[14] This was a retreat justified by arguments about women's proper place and their innate need for marriage, children and housework. It was, however, driven by the need to ensure that the men being demobbed had jobs to come back to and would not, for example, fall prey to any pesky revolutionary ideas.

To point out how the needs of capitalism have shaped women's oppression is not, of course, to minimise the achievements of women's struggles against it. However, an understanding of the historical nature of women's oppression under capitalism does lead to particular conclusions about how we can continue to fight it.

The struggle against women's oppression today

Women's oppression is part of the system of exploitation by the ruling class, and under capitalism, the particular form of women's oppression we face is part of the way in which the bourgeoisie exploits the proletariat. It is not innate to the human condition nor an inevitable facet of relations in all societies between men and women. What this means is that in fighting this oppression, it is not the case that all women have more interests in common with each other than they do with any men. On the contrary, because women's oppression is part of class exploitation, proletarian women have more interests in common with proletarian men than we do with women who are members of the bourgeoisie.

This means that increases in the numbers of women represented on the boards of major companies do little for most women, and that the sort of feminist campaigns that focus on these as advances against women's oppression are rather missing the point. There is no trickle-down effect, whereby the successes of a minority of bourgeois women lead to advances for women as a whole against our exploitation. It's also worth noting that the women who make it to CEO are often no more understanding of the particular issues facing the women who work for them than their male counterparts would be. One example is the infamous book, *Lean In*, by Sheryl Sandberg,

CEO of Facebook, which implies that if women are discriminated against in the workplace it's their fault for not trying hard enough. Marissa Mayer, celebrated in some quarters when she became CEO of Yahoo while being five months' pregnant, is another. Her decision to take only two weeks' maternity leave and her edict banning Yahoo's employees from working from home show that a female leader does not automatically mean female-friendly policies. Mayer, by the way, juggles her childcare responsibilities and the need to be at work for long hours every day by having a nursery in her office; a perk not supplied to everyone working at Yahoo.

The understanding that women's oppression is part of class oppression also has implications for the position of men in the movement fighting it. It is often assumed that men should have no or very little place in the struggle against women's oppression. This makes sense, of course, if you think that men themselves are the problem, but less so when we realise that the issue is not individual men, but capitalism. Just as when with other oppressions, such as racism or homophobia, we understand that these are strategies to divide the working class and set us against each other rather than against our class enemies, so women and men need to stand together against women's oppression.

In order to do so, men would have to give up the advantages which they do have over women in the current sexist system, from higher pay to the right to do most of the talking in political meetings. These marginal advantages do not, however, outweigh proletarian men's class interests in overthrowing the class oppression of which women's oppression is a part.

It is of course right and necessary that women should lead this struggle – the women's movement has to be a place where women's voices do not get drowned out by men – and in order to cope with the sexism we face, women have to retain the absolute right to women-only spaces when we need them. As Tony Cliff said, however, 'A white revolutionary must be more extreme in opposing racism than a black revolutionary. A gentile revolutionary must oppose anti-Semitism more strongly than any Jew. A male revolutionary must be completely intolerant of any harassment or belittling of women. We must be the tribune of the oppressed.'[16] It is the job of all of us, women and men, to fight women's oppression, and it is in the interests of all of us that we win.

Notes

1. Laura Bates, *Everyday Sexism* (London 2014).

2. http://www.ihollaback.org/

3. On brain development and the relationship between brain and mind, see Steven Rose, *The 21st-Century Brain Explaining, Mending and Manipulating the Mind* (London 2006) and Alison Gopnik, Andrew Meltzoff and Patricia Kuhl, *How Babies Think: The Science of Childhood* (London 2001).

4. For a detailed takedown of the idea that men just don't understand basic communication (like the word 'no' in sexual situations), see Deborah Cameron, *The Myth of Mars and Venus* (Oxford 2007).

5. Cordelia Fine, *Delusions of Gender: The Real Science Behind Sex Differences* (London 2010).

6. A well-known example of the claim that modern-day hunter-gatherer societies give us a view on to the Paleolithic, and of the problems with it, is Allan R. Holmberg in his 1950 book about the Sirionó people of the Beni, in Bolivia, *Nomads of the Longbow*. Holmberg thought that the material and cultural poverty of the Sirionó he met showed 'man in the raw state of nature', but in fact they were the scattered survivors of attacks by ranchers and the Bolivian military, and devastating smallpox and flu epidemics. 'It was as if he had come across refugees from a Nazi concentration camp, and concluded that they belonged to a culture that had always been barefoot and starving'; Charles C. Mann, *1491: New Revelations of the Americas Before Columbus* (New York 2006), p.10. In fact, of course, no modern society, however different in appearance from that of the West, can escape the impact of capitalism.

7. For a recent example of the first type of argument, see Paul Seabright, *The War of the Sexes: How Conflict and Cooperation Have Shaped Men and Women from Prehistory to the Present* (Princeton 2012), p.17. Others disagree with the sexual coercion hypothesis, while

agreeing that hunting provided the most valued food, and was mostly carried out by men, see for example Chris Harman, *A People's History of the World*, 2nd ed. (London 2008), p.8.

8. Roger Lewin, *Bones of Contention: Controversies in the Search for Human Origins* (New York 1987), pp.315-17.

9. Frederick Engels, *The Origins of the Family, Private Property and the State* (London 1972).

10. Bernhard Brosius, '*From Cayonu to Catalhöyük: Emergence and development of an egalitarian society*', (Munich 2004), http://www.urkommunismus.de/catal-hueyuek_en.pdf.

11. Mann, *1491*, pp.369-78.

12. Ibid, p.373.

13. Lindsey German, *Material Girls. Women, men and work* (London 2007), p.55.

14. Betty Friedan, *The Feminine Mystique* (New York 1963).

15. http://www.huffingtonpost.com/lisa-belkin/marissa-mayer-work-from-home-yahoo-rule_b_2750256.html

16. Tony Cliff, *Marxism at the Millennium* (London 2000), p.50.

3. Race, class and women's oppression

Feyzi Ismail

Under neoliberalism, women face heightened levels of exploitation and oppression, black people and ethnic minorities are scapegoated, Muslims are seen as obstacles to so-called British values and security, and most people live under conditions of increasing precarity, insecurity and intensification of work. Between these different oppressions, capitalism facilitates, encourages and thrives on divisions between people. How we overcome these different oppressions is a question of strategy.

An understanding of the sources of oppression, and the way different oppressions work in capitalist society, is crucial. The recognition that these oppressions need to be located as part of a wider struggle to change an exploitative system, is also crucial. New generations of feminists search for an analysis that links women's inequality to a wider critique of capitalist society. At the same time, we are witnessing increasing rejection of racism and war, and increasing concern over refugees, the free movement of labour, the global financial crisis and its impact the world over.

Attempts to understand the interrelationship between race, class and women's oppression are not new. They came out of concrete struggles, first against slavery in the US, and then within the movements against racism and sexism. Second-wave feminism in the US, Britain and elsewhere emerged from a period of struggle motivated primarily in the first instance by anti-racism and anti-imperialism: the civil-rights movement and the anti-Vietnam War movements in the 1960s.

Exploitation and oppression

Angela Davis, who was a prominent Communist Party leader and Black Panther supporter in the US, argued in *Women, Race and Class* how the multidimensional role of black women, and particularly women's lives under slavery, had to be analysed firstly in terms of their role as workers: 'the slave woman was first a full-time worker for her owner, and only incidentally a wife, mother and homemaker.'[1] As workers, they suffered the same oppression as men.

But they suffered additional exploitation and oppression as women, and as black women. Davis gives the example of how when the abolition of the international slave trade began to threaten the expansion of the cotton industry, black women slaves who could give birth to many children were coveted, because they could grow the slave labour force naturally. These women would then be vulnerable to all kinds of sexual coercion; Davis argues that 'rape, in fact, was an uncamouflaged expression of the slaveholder's economic mastery and the overseer's control over black women as workers.'[2]

Rape is arguably one of the most destructive and devastating manifestations of women's oppression. But rape also had a toxic racial component in the US during slavery, as a key weapon in maintaining white supremacy. Davis argues that rape was 'an essential dimension of the social relations between slave master and slave' and involved the routine rape of black slave women by their white masters.[3] The goal was to destroy women's ability to resist. Rape survived slavery and continues to be used as a weapon of war to humiliate whole populations.

Anti-racism and second-wave feminism

This analysis – of the particular forms of oppression faced by black women – was beginning to be raised during second-wave feminism in the 1960s and 1970s. While second-wave feminism was inspired by the struggles against racism, it was also a reaction to the fact that inside those struggles, including in the civil rights movement, women's voices weren't being heard. Even within the Black Panther Party, which had a majority-women membership, the leadership was mainly men, and sexism wasn't being taken seriously.

As second-wave women's movements developed in the 1970s, even though many of those involved were committed anti-racist activists and supported the anti-colonial struggles in Asia and Africa, there were criticisms that the experiences of black women in particular and the multiple oppressions they faced were being neglected and marginalised. The argument was that it was *white* women's experiences that the feminist movements were actually representing. The discrimination – when it came to employment, housing, access to services and so on – and the violence and abuse that black women faced, including in the epidemic of sterilisation abuse against black, Native American, and Latina women in the US at the time, were neither being understood nor challenged.

The context in which these struggles were taking place is significant. All of these movements coincided with a period of massive radicalisation at the end of the 1960s, peaking in 1968. The struggle against racism in the US combined with opposition to the Vietnam War to produce a genuine social crisis in the US. France was paralysed by a general strike of up to ten million workers, which had been detonated by a militant student movement. And this radicalisation wasn't only happening in the West. Around the world there were massive movements challenging the status quo, which in many countries spilled over into levels of working-class struggle not seen since the 1930s. In other countries, there were armed insurgencies, including in Asia and Latin America, and these struggles had political, economic and cultural effects that permeated the whole of those societies.

In this context, it was easy to see the limitations of of campaigning for purely formal, political equality, however important. Second-wave feminism's demands challenged social and economic inequality, which was felt in much lower wages for women, and a situation where women carried the overwhelming burden of childcare and housework.

One of the biggest impetuses to the women's movement in Britain was the Dagenham strike over equal pay in 1968. When the work of the women sewing machinists at the Ford factory was categorised as 'less skilled' than their male counterparts, they walked out of the factory for three weeks and completely halted production. They refused to be paid less than men for the same kind of work. The strike led to the Equal Pay Act of 1970, and undoubtedly helped strengthen the movement.

In this way, the interaction of mass struggles generalised into real challenges to the system, radicalising the women's movements both in the US and in Britain. By the mid-1970s, however, the working-class and left movements had begun to retreat. The movements against oppression also began to experience fragmentation, and partly as a consequence, began to be contained.

The momentum generated by the French working class, for example, was blocked by an agreement between de Gaulle and the trade union leaders, who were granted concessions and a general election in return for getting those millions of workers back to work. The last major revolutionary upsurge, at least in Europe, was Portugal in 1974, which came just after the overthrow of the social democratic leader Allende in Chile in 1973. The defeat of Allende and the neoliberal reforms imposed in Chile could be considered the turning point during this period that marked the beginning of the decline of struggle, of working class parties, of the defeat of trade unions, and the rise of neoliberalism.

Black and white feminism
Under these circumstances, in which struggles were effectively absorbed by the system and the state was using strategies of incorporation, a single-issue consciousness began to emerge. It was argued that each oppression must be fought separately. The cross-fertilisation and the convergence of the movements in the late 1960s began to be reversed. Struggles against racism and women's oppression began to diverge and the challenge to the system as a

whole was weakened. At the same time, black women also began to organise separately. One prominent organisation, the Combahee River Collective, was formed in the mid-1970s by a collective of black feminists, some of whom were veterans of the Black Panther Party. They felt that white women feminists' sole focus on gender was problematic and argued for an ideological separation from white feminism. They also felt that ranking race, class and women's oppression showed a misunderstanding of the multiple and interlocking nature of oppression. Their defining statement, issued in 1977, described a vision for black feminism as opposing all forms of oppression, including sexuality, gender identity, class, disability and age.

Nevertheless, despite the understanding of the nature of oppression demonstrated by the Combahee River Collective and others, the early 1970s is notable for the beginnings of the rise of so-called identity politics. The vision of identity politics wasn't so much about changing the world through class struggle or overturning relations of exploitation, but was rather about self-definition and 'focusing on our own oppression'.[4] Within this view of oppression, asserting your position and your identity was paramount, and change tended to be conceived in terms of language, law and culture.

For large sections of the movement, mirroring versions of Black Nationalism that tended to see white people as the problem, men had become the problem, not an exploitative and oppressive social system. By the early 1980s, certainly in Britain, this kind of identity politics had found a home in the Labour Party. This was important as it meant that it became part of the strategy of reformism: the point was not to change the system but to change legislation and, crucially, the language used by the state and within interpersonal relationships

This is not to argue, of course, that issues of language and the law were unimportant. The legal position of women and the language used about them were real reflections of the lived experience of racism and sexism, and this continues to be the case. The concept of of intersectionality gained prominence partly in response to real issues of fragmentation in the movements that emerged in the 1970s. It sought to overcome that fragmentation by mapping the intersection or connections between race, class and gender in all their complexity.

Intersectionality and its limits

Kimberlé Crenshaw argued in a seminal paper in the late 1980s that black women were discriminated against in ways that often didn't fit neatly into either category of racism or sexism. Rather, they experienced discrimination as a combination of both. She argued that 'black women's experience of sexism is shaped equally by racism and class inequality and is therefore different in certain respects from the experience of white, middle-class women.'[5] Moreover, in assuming that the experiences of middle-class white women were representative, a false unity and solidarity among women was presupposed. The legal system, for example, would render black women in particular invisible, because the unspoken reference point for claims against sexism would be white women, just as the unspoken reference point against racism would be that faced by black men.[6] Theorising all of this, and using it in the legal sphere, was a step forward.

Class was also theorised as one among other sources of oppression and, consistent with an intersectional approach, was not to be privileged over the others; the point was that there are multiple oppressions: to fight one oppression, other forms of oppression needed to be considered. If you're a black woman, or a black, working-class woman, or a black, lesbian, disabled, working-class woman, understanding that complexity and theorising about how those oppressions work together is crucial.

The limitation of much intersectionality theory, however, is that it tends to see the interrelation between oppressions in a descriptive and formal way, using categories of privilege and identity rather than rather than locating the origins and causes of oppression and concretely analysing the distinct ways in which oppression and exploitation interact. As a result, it fell short of providing a strategy to overcome oppression. Martha Gimenez noted that identities were forms of resistance when they were linked to social movements, but were susceptible to becoming 'legitimating identities' or identities that could be, as she argues, 'harnessed by the state in narrow legal and political boundaries that rule out other forms of political self-understanding.'[7]

This implied a kind of structural determinism: that your identity should determine your particular interests, your politics and your experiences. Intersectionality assumed the existence of common interests and ideologies based on identity – gender, race or ethnicity – when in fact the oppressions that affect people's lives are generated by wider society and always deeply structured by class. While intersctionality is grappling with a crucial set of problems, its tendency not to locate oppression directly in the dynamics of modern capitalism inhibits its ability to adequately challenge the fragmentation experienced by movements against oppression over the last several decades.

Worse still, intersectionality morphed into black and white feminism, opening up the possibility of seeing these struggles as separate, contradictory and at odds with one another. The conclusion could be drawn that black and white women could not struggle alongside each other, and that they had to organise separately, because white women could never understand the racism experienced by black women.

The uses of racism and sexism

Racism came out of the early development of capitalism, and the emergence of class society, justifying the slave trade and colonialism. In pre-capitalist societies racism did not exist as biological discrimination; there was cultural discrimination but biological discrimination emerged later as an ideology to justify imperialism on the one hand, but also to keep workers divided.

Divisions along gender lines have also had their uses for capitalism. Sexism and the division of labour within the family – and the fact that the family encodes ideas of the woman as carer – meant that a new generation of workers could brought up without the state having to invest in this crucial necessity. The state might invest in the health and education of the young, but replenishing the labour market and performing the unpaid labour to care for the future labour force would be done privately, and by women. While production is socialised, reproduction is privatised. Society then judges women according to whether they are prepared to perform this complex set of roles that is demanded of them.

It is because of the role that women play in society that austeriy impacts so harshly on them. Since the Second World War in particular, gains had been won that improved women's lives, providing childcare, crèches, child benefit and so on. In the last several decades, many of those gains have been rolled back. We are back to a world in which the family continues to be regarded as the core institution in which society reproduces itself, 'family values' are glorified and women continue bear the brunt of that labour.

Women's role in the workplace, is often regarded as secondary. The fact that many women leave work to have children means that for capitalists they are unreliable workers. There has been an important critique that middle-class, white women have dominated the women's movement. But the more fundamental question is what structures these oppressions in the first place. Here an understanding of women's position in the capitalist labour market and the family as the site of social reproduction, is essential.

War and the new racism

In terms of our own struggles now, against austerity and war, we need to consider how to develop a coherent strategy to link different struggles. To do this, we have to reject narratives of the likes of Sheryl Sandberg and Nike's Girl Power, which suggest that women's oppression is a thing of the past, or has been overcome by the fact that we have women CEOs. We also have to reject a feminism that ignores class exploitation and racism; one that is ignorant of the experiences of poor women, or women in the developing world. Once again, we need to theorise oppression that isn't merely legalistic or one-dimensional but genuinely unravels the way in which different oppressions impact on each other. For example, we need to understand the ways in which the War on Terror has generated a wave of Islamophobia, affecting the lives of Muslim women in particular. Simply seeing the use of the veil as mainly a symbol of women's oppression is to misunderstand the nature of anti-Muslim racism.

There is no escaping the fact that women's lives are structured by the great forces of neoliberalism and imperialism. To chart a way forward for liberation isn't about reducing questions of oppression to those of class, but of analysing how these forces shape our societies and our lives.

We live in a moment of challenges and opportunites. In Britain, we have the most left-wing Labour leadership in generations. We have had a series of mass movements against war and against austerity that have made a considerable impact on public opinion. There is a deep desire for an end to the neoliberal regime. The point is to identify the ways in which the system articulates gender in order to reproduce itself, and to develop a sophisticated critique of oppression that will encourage resistance against it that will be effective. If women feel the brunt of the attacks in austerity Britain, they are correspondingly crucial agents in the struggle against it. Strategically placed at the heart of politically sensitive public services, central to many workforces and trade unions but also the key to the modern family, it is impossible to conceive of a radical movement for change that is not largely led by women.

The reality and the historical experience has been that most radical assault on sexism and racist oppression took place in the 1960s when people were challenging the system as a whole. We need to put system change back onto the agenda once again.

Notes

1. Stampp, K. (1956) cited in Davis, A. (1981[1983]). *Women, Race and Class*. New York: Random House.
2. Davis, A. (1981[1983]).
3. Ibid.
4. Combahee River Collective: 'A Black Feminist Statement'. In: Freedman, E.B. (ed.) (2007) *The Essential Feminist Reader*. New York: The Modern Library.
5. Smith, S. (2013) Black Feminism and Intersectionality, *International Socialist Review*, 91.
6. Crenshaw, K. (1989) Demarginalizing the Intersection of Race and Sex: A Black Feminist Critique of Anti-discrimination Doctrine, Feminist Theory and Anti-racist Politics. *University of Chicago Legal Forum*, 1(8): 139-167.
7. Giminez, M. (2001) Marxism and Class, Gender and Race: Rethinking the Trilogy. *Race, Gender and Class*, 8(2): 23-33.

4. Marxism and feminism

Lindsey German

Marxism and feminism have had a relationship which has been described famously as an 'unhappy marriage'. While those who were attracted to the feminist ideas of the 1960s and early 1970s often had a close relationship to Marxism, the experience of the last few decades has been that the two have led largely separate lives. The various Marxist analyses of oppression and the various feminist ones tended to develop along different paths.

However, while there was been an acceptance of mainstream feminism at many institutional levels within capitalist society, it has also become increasingly obvious that the position of women is not improving overall. Indeed, in a globalised, neoliberal world, women are facing levels of exploitation and oppression which are both interlinked and heightened by the nature of that society. The need for migration, precarity, insecurity and intensification of work, all impact heavily on women.

This in turn has led to an increased interest in feminism, and in the need to explain and understand the nature of women's oppression, as new generations of feminists search for analysis which links women's equality to a wider critique of capitalist society. In a world where women's oppression remains a central feature of society, the need for an analysis which locates the fight against oppression in the context of a fight against class society is more and more pressing. In such a context, Marxism has an important contribution to make in terms of analysing oppression and its links with exploitation.

Marxism's recognition of oppression

Marxism is a theory of human emancipation, sometimes called a universal theory, which attempts to explain all oppression and exploitation in relation to class society. This has often led to the charge from some feminists that it is a 'reductionist' theory - that it reduces all such questions to ones of class, rather than considering the specific nature of women's oppression. A second feminist criticism, and in some way connected to this, is that Marxism denies the agency of individual men as the perpetrators of oppression, because it sees oppression as created by class. It therefore denies the need to organise against men as well as against capitalism.

Both involve a misunderstanding of what Marxist class analysis is about. It starts from the understanding that capitalist society is divided into classes, but this is not necessarily a straightforward division. Marx sees class as an economic relationship, defined by individuals' relationship to the means of production. There are two main contending classes, who on the one hand exploit and on the other hand are exploited. This in itself might be a fairly straightforward picture, with the main classes being either the working class or the ruling class. But there are both divisions within the working class, and also a number of other, smaller groups or classes who have some relationship to one or the other of the main classes.

Marxist theory is centred on an economic theory

of exploitation, in which the surplus produced through work is expropriated by those who control the production of wealth and its distribution. Yet it is not simply an economic theory. It also aims to explain political and social divisions in terms of the needs of an exploitative system, the way in which divisions within society are created and recreated to suit the needs of this system, and the extent to which ideas and actions themselves develop as a result of the economic relationships in society.

While the working class is the exploited class, it is not a uniform class. It has divisions in terms of gender, race, sexuality, nationality, skill, and many others. These divisions also often cut across classes: all women suffer a specific oppression as women; all black people suffer a specific oppression because of their race.

The recognition of that oppression is crucial for Marxists and socialists, and the recognition that it needs to be specifically located and fought against as part of a wider struggle to change an exploitative and oppressive system is also key. The strength and enduring power of the great movements of the 1960s are precisely that they did this. In so doing, they created a situation where the working-class movement had to take on board the understanding of oppression and the need to overcome it even within the working class.

However, those of us who locate oppression within class society also argue that it is only in the process of fighting to overcome class society that the movement to end oppression can really succeed. Only when class relations of production, which help create and recreate oppressions precisely in order to divide those who are exploited, are overthrown, can full equality and freedom from all divisions really be achieved.

This analysis allows us to integrate the struggles against oppression into the wider fight against class society. Far from reducing oppression to class, this broadens out not just the analysis of oppression but points to ways of fighting against it. Developing a class analysis of oppression which goes beyond locating that oppression but also views that oppression through an understanding of its link to class society and the necessity to overthrow it, enables Marxism to have a much more extensive view of oppression and class.

Revolutionaries and the struggle for reforms

To designate sexism and racism as products of class society can of course lead to a passive sense that nothing can be done to challenge them in the here and now. This tendency towards abstraction and passivity has in truth always been a strand within the left and working-class movements, and not just over these questions. For example, even great socialists like William Morris sometimes argued against strikes because they only achieved small wage rises, when what was needed was the overthrow of the system.

But anyone whose socialism remains at this level of abstraction will not get very far. Instead, the need is to link the immediate campaigns and struggles of working people with the emancipatory idea of socialism and the full transformation of society. So, for many socialists it has always been important to draw connections between the immediate fights to improve people's lives, whether over economic issues like wages, or political issues of democracy or supposedly 'individual' issues such as divorce or abortion, with the long-term goal to change society and end exploitation and oppression. That is why the German Marxist Rosa Luxemburg wrote over 100 years ago about the need to fight for reforms in order to help create the conditions for revolution. Indeed, she argued that revolutionaries were the most consistent fighters for reforms because they set them in the wider context.

Those reforms include campaigning for laws and other sanctions to deal with issues such as rape, domestic violence, sexual harassment and many others which are the reality of far too many women's lives. Individual men perpetrate these acts and should be condemned accordingly. While we are all shaped by social forces which we do not choose, we are in a position to make choices about our behaviour, our treatment of other people and the decisions we make in our lives. But we also cannot ignore the social context in which women are objectified and subject to violence, and this goes far beyond the individual actions of men.

So campaigning on these issues is not at all incompatible with an overview of society which says that class society creates women's oppression, it deliberately acts at certain times to strengthen or aid oppressive forces and that the possibility of ending oppression lies in the overthrow of this society.

Women's oppression, capitalism and the family

When we talk about women's oppression and its relationship to class society, it is of course the most enduring oppression, having existed throughout different class societies (as Elaine Graham-Leigh explains earlier). Under capitalism, its particular nature is tied up with the family and the reproduction of labour power - what is often referred to as social reproduction.

Capitalism constantly searches for fresh sources of labour, bringing in new groups - who previously had not been involved in paid work - as reserves of labour who can be exploited. In particular, it needs young, fresh workers to replenish older and more tired workers. Thus, capital has an interest in ensuring the safe and efficient reproduction of the next generation of workers, at as little cost to itself as possible. The privatised family, which teaches, cares for, trains, socialises and nurtures the new generation of workers does so at great cost to individual parents and other family members in terms of unpaid labour, including emotional labour, and financial outlay, and at relatively little cost to the capitalist state. It therefore helps reproduce new workers at 18 or 21 who are skilled, socialised, literate and numerate, and who contribute their surplus value to the wealth of capital.

This does not necessarily have to take place in the privatised family, but it is a system which has, despite its inherent flaws, worked well both economically and socially, and has been a major force for stability within society. It ensures the reproduction of the existing generation of workers and most importantly the next generation at very little cost to the capitalist class and, despite the weaknesses of the family and the horrors which sometimes lie within it, is a relatively efficient and cheap way of doing so. A recent survey by the ONS estimated that £1 trillion worth equivalent of paid work is carried out within the home and family unpaid, the majority of it by women. The need to maintain the family system is central to capital, which provides a legal, educational and social system which helps to keep it going.

This system has built within it the systematic oppression of women, through women's domestic role. Women, despite their role as full participants in the labour market, still carry out the bulk of domestic labour as well. While they work less hours in paid work than men, they work more hours overall if paid and unpaid work are both taken into account. The family is often far from the idealized picture beloved of advertisers and right-wing politicians. It is the main site of violence against women, including being the place where the majority of murders take place, and also hides widespread abuse of children. The existence of the family in turn has an impact on attitudes to women, reinforcing low pay, sexual harassment and abuse.

It can be argued that capital does not need to resort to a separate system of oppression such as patriarchy to explain the position of women: it is locked into a system of privatised social reproduction which systematically places women in an oppressed role. The contradiction between socialised production and privatised reproduction is the contradiction between the ability of working people to come together collectively and organise, and the private responsibility for childcare and other domestic labour which is the family, and for which family members alone are held responsible if it fails in some way. It is impossible to separate this, in turn, from the treatment of women, whether in the home, in work or in wider society, helping to define the sorts of jobs they do, the levels of pay they receive, and the stereotypes of women which still exist. The relationship between this system of oppression and the exploitation of wage labour - both male and female- is the key to understanding the oppression of women within capitalism.

The fight for women's liberation

The development of capitalism itself changed the nature of the family and of women's oppression. It also raised many questions of equality and individual freedom, including ideas of women's equality, as people struggled to escape the yoke of the old feudal society, with its lack of freedom, its stultifying ideas and its highly repressive religious and political superstructure. As early as the English and French revolutions of the seventeenth and eighteenth centuries, ideas of women's equality, of free love and of the potential for individual women to change their situation and try to achieve equality began to emerge. Women's right to education, to work outside the home, and to achieve full political and legal equality became key issues around which women organised at different times.

At the beginning of the twentieth century, a movement of women erupted around the demand for women to have the right to vote, in other words, demanding political equality with men. The demand was fuelled by the injustice of women's situation, and by the intransigence of a Liberal government, but it also reflected huge changes in women's lives and consciousness. The struggle for the vote led to eventual success, in Britain following a world war which changed women's lives forever. However, it was rapidly apparent that women achieving the vote, although important, left many key social and economic questions untouched, and that real equality and freedom still eluded them. It took another world war to further break down barriers to women's work and education, and to begin to change attitudes to the family and women's sexual role.

The clash between on the one hand women's increased public involvement in work and education, and on the other hand the persistence of traditional attitudes towards women, led to the emergence of what is now widely termed Second Wave feminism: the women's liberation movement of the late 1960s which emerged in the US and then spread elsewhere. Recognising the limitations of purely political equality, its demands challenged the social and economic inequality which decreed that women's wages were much lower than men's and that women carried the overwhelming burden of childcare and housework.

The impact of the 1960s and 1970s on women's lives in countries such as the US and Britain was immense: laws changed, new areas of work opened up, attitudes towards women altered. The movement helped usher in greater social and economic equality. But fundamental change in terms of complete equality proved elusive. The fight for women's liberation came up against the barrier of class society: the right to work alongside men became the right to be exploited alongside men; the right to freer sexuality and freedom from prejudice suffered, as everything to do with sex was turned into a commodity.

Connecting Marxism and feminism

The points made by thinkers in the Marxist tradition, that the nature of capitalist society prevented genuine equality for women or any other oppressed group precisely because capitalist production ensures the continuation of privatised reproduction, remain true. This is despite the very real gains which have been made for women under capitalism. And even these gains can find themselves under attack, whether in terms of wages and conditions at work, or over issues such as abortion and reproductive rights. We have seen, for example, the recent attempt by the Polish government to limit even further abortion in that country, which was met by a women's strike (supported by many men) that successfully defeated the move.

The need to go beyond capitalist society to achieve women's liberation does not mean ignoring current attacks, or counterposing a long-term glowing egalitarian future with the harsh reality of the present. It means that the fight for women's liberation has to be both about defending and extending existing gains, while always arguing that permanent liberation for not only women but the whole of humanity is only possible in a society based on production for need, not profit.

This directly connects to a critique of different sorts of feminism, and it leads to an understanding of why there is such a schism between those who see feminism simply in terms of individual women's advancement and those who see it as connected to wider social change. Capital in the age of neoliberalism is happy to accept a small number of women making it to the top, as long as they are committed to maintaining the status quo. So while there is the prospect of the first woman US president this year, she is no friend of working women. She accepts the inequality agenda of Wall Street, is an inveterate warmonger and is determined to enforce worse conditions on millions of workers, including women. The British prime minister, Theresa May, espouses conservative social values and promotes policies which attack workers' rights.

Feminism and women's liberation are not about individual empowerment, feminist consumerism (the right sort of T shirt), or getting individual women into 'top' positions. They are not primarily about getting women's images on banknotes, or adopting 'role models' whose success is usually based on the employment of other women to carry out their domestic labour and childcare. They are about linking the question of women's oppression to other inequalities and oppressions: racism, imperialism and the consequences of working-class exploitation.

It is here that the connection between Marxism and feminism can be made. The fight against capital takes many forms, including the fight for women's full equality. Increasing numbers of people are recognizing that different issues and campaigns are connected, that there needs to be a system change in order to deal with the inequalities and wrongs which afflict the vast majority of us. To achieve this will take a movement based on class, but one which is informed and fully participated in by the movements against oppression. The possibility of achieving this may appear daunting, but it is also more necessary than ever if we are to achieve equality.

About the authors

Katherine Connelly
Katherine Connelly is a writer and historian. She led school-student strikes in the British anti-war movement in 2003, co-ordinated the Emily Wilding Davison Memorial Campaign in 2013 and is a leading member of Counterfire. Her book, *Sylvia Pankhurst: Suffragette, Socialist and Scourge of Empire* is published by Pluto Press.

Elaine Graham-Leigh
Elaine Graham-Leigh is a writer, historian and campaigner, focusing in particular on issues of climate change and social justice. Her book, *A Diet of Austerity: Class, Food and Climate Change*, is published by Zero Books.

Feyzi Ismail
Feyzi Ismail teaches at SOAS, University of London, and is an active UCU member. She is a contributor to *The Assault on Universities: A Manifesto for Resistance*, and has published various articles on politics and development in Nepal and South Asia, neoliberalism and resistance.

Lindsey German
As national convenor of the Stop the War Coalition, Lindsey German was a key organiser of the largest demonstration, and one of the largest mass movements, in British history. Her books include *Material Girls: Women, Men and Work*, *Sex, Class and Socialism*, *A People's History of London* (with John Rees) and *How a Century of War Changed the Lives of Women*.

Further reading

Lindsey German
Material Girls: Women, Men and Work
Sex, Class and Socialism
How a Century of War Changed the Lives of Women

Katherine Connelly
Sylvia Pankhurst, Suffragette, Socialist and Scourge of Empire

Friedrich Engels
Origins of the Family, Private Property and the State

Lisa Vogel
Marxism and the Oppression of Women

Hester Eisenstein
Feminism Seduced: How Global Elites Use Women's Labour and Ideas to Exploit the World

Heather Brown
Marx on Gender and the Family: A Critical Study

Cordelia Fine
Delusions of Gender: The Real Science Behind Sex Differences

Angela Davis
Women, Race and Class

Help us remake socialist politics for the 21st century

Counterfire builds the movements against war, austerity, racism and climate change.

Corbyn's victory has helped the left and we need to stay mobilised to support him. We think fundamental change comes from below, and that socialists need to get organised to help make this happen. We want to see a left that can make a real difference to the world and we are growing.

Counterfire.org is one of the best-read websites on the radical left, and we are now producing a regular free tabloid in the same spirit. We have Counterfire groups across the country and they need your help and ideas to make change happen.

Help us remake socialist politics for the twenty-first century. Join us, we are stronger together.

www.counterfire.org/join